The Wages of Goodness

Poems by
Michael Blumenthal

University of Missouri Press
Columbia and London

Blumenthal, Michael.
    The wages of goodness : poems / by Michael Blumenthal.
        p.   cm.
    ISBN 0-8262-0832-0 (alk. paper). — ISBN 0-8262-0833-9 (pbk. :
alk. paper)
    I. Title.
PS3552.L849W3   1992
811'.54—dc20   91-40023
                                                                       CIP

C.1

∞™ This paper meets the minimum requirements of
the American National Standard for Permanence of Paper
for Printed Library Materials, Z39.48, 1984.

Acknowledgments

The author wishes to thank the John Simon Guggenheim Memorial Foundation
for its generous support during the 1988–1989 academic year, when many of the
poems in this volume were first written and revised.

The following poems, some revised since their original publication, appeared in the
indicated magazines and periodicals, to whose editors the author owes his grati-
tude for their generosity and confidence: "God Loves You, and So Do I," *The
American Scholar;* "Letters Floating around Ellis Island" and "The Apprentice,"
The Colorado Review; "The Connoisseur of Starts," *Lines Review* (Scotland);
"Poem for My Father at 85" and "Yin and Yang," *The Nation;* "And the Wages of
Goodness Are Not Assured," "First Snow: Cambridge, Massachusetts," and
"Ordinary Heartbreaks," *Poetry;* "United Jewish Appeal," *Tikkun.*

Designer: Elizabeth Fett
Typesetter: Connell-Zeko Type & Graphics
Printer: Thomson-Shore, Inc.
Binder: Thomson-Shore, Inc.
Typeface: Sabon and Perpetua

for Isabelle and Noah

Gracias à la vida,
que me ha dado tanto

Contents

The Wages
of Goodness

I

The Wages of Love

The business of love is cruelty which,
by our wills,
> *we transform*
>> *to live together.*
>>> —William Carlos Williams
>>> "The Ivy Crown"

The Connoisseur of Starts

He loved the quick and hot commencements best:
The rip and flow of tides in early spring.
He loved the inklings most. As for the rest,
They seemed a paltry sequel to the brisk morning.
Cacophonous birds twittered in the light,
Wild chirpings from an elemental source.
And what remained of singing through the night
Seemed like the broken canter of a limping horse.
Trees blossomed, but before their leaves had turned
He'd found other landscapes, other regions.
And couldn't warm himself where once he'd burned
As the initiate of countless legions.
But now he felt his mastery extending—
In fits and starts: the connoisseur of endings.

Aubade

A silvered light against my hand
as we awoke, the diddled drift
of air above the sheets,
a tenderness of lips. I watched
your eyes remake the night
toward day again, I heard
the birds applaud the fading dew.
All that we said last night
remains: an ornament
with words, a song,
a whispered wish,
and lovelier than true.

The Happiest Day of Your Life
for D.

You were in Chicago. It was September.
You had met a woman in a bar,
and, love being, as Freud said, lust
overlaid with tenderness, took her home.
You had a late dinner, over candles,
good music, expensive scotch,
and, with every delicious morsel
of the evening, your body rose
like a fast-frame flower, and you felt
the divine happiness of a desired, still-
untainted thing about to happen, the imagined
and the real flowing into each other
like happy rivers. Like a pitcher
carrying a huge lead into the late innings,
you could afford to be tranquil, slow,
experimental even (here a forkball, there
a change-up), knowing it was just a matter of time
before the happy embrace of bodies over the mound
to which you had repeatedly risen. Finally,
it began, and like one of the great explorers
coming by accident or intention to a new place,
you found in each tuft of the landscape
a blessed newness, you whisked joyfully
into a terrain where every feather and blade
cried out to you: new! new! and your mouth,
your fingers, your unimpedable cock, knew again
the great, temporary happiness of death defeated.
All night things turned this way (fucking, sleeping,
fucking, sleeping) and, when morning came,
you had reached the other side of the island
of your discovering, and the sun was rising,
and you kissed her good-bye over coffee
and went off to get a Sunday paper,
which you sat reading, alone, in the
bright, morning light along Lake Michigan,
the only thing fluttering around you the sound of birds,
the pages of newsprint in your hand, turning.

The Apprentice

His whole life had been movement,
so now he decided to remain in one place.
He decided to leave in this one place
his hate and his love, his self-loathing
and his beautiful ambivalence. He stood
in that single place of slanted light
against all impulse, like a deer
that had lifted its tail so often
it had fatigued of its own fleeing
and stood now, against all enemies,
in the dappled light of its original stillness.
All day, the huge dialectic of hate and love
ran through him, whispering *go, flee,*
shaping its ornate battalion of fears
and abandonments into a single map,
waving the boats in from the busy harbor
as if to board, but finally taking from them
only a small bounty of clams and shells
and waving the good captain on
to his pearly islands of lusts and departures.
Soon, all his comings and goings, his loves
and his violent loathings, were like the weight
of a huge pendulum: the arc of each swinging
growing shorter and shorter. Not knowing it,
he had become the field of his own forces,
the calm of his own turbulence. He turned,
now, the hands of desire and longing
into his own deep center. He fell asleep
on his own ship, dreaming the boats on
in the busy harbor of goings and arrivals.
All the magnificent animals of his bestiary
were terrestrial now, and the trees opened,
and his true love came to him in the luminous dark.

The Young

So here they are:
they who have not yet mastered
the great, sexual longing,
and who can blame them? Bone
by distended bone, flesh by flesh,
how they would love to be joined,
how they would love to escape
the terrible takeover of the singular self.
Riding each other in dim corners—
superior, disdainful, pitying us,
they hang over the guardrails
like posters asking us to a summer concert
long sold out, like lights
from already extinguished stars.
But we, too, have something to tell them,
we who have arrived tear-strewn,
restrained, enviably calm
at our dignified lot, who have grown so slowly
into our first box of flesh and deep breathing
and are seated here now, on *Direction
Port de la Chapelle* of the Paris Metro,
trembling in our separate suits of flesh,
telling them how it is.

Matinee

It could almost be an affair, this slinking off,
mid-week, on a bright, April afternoon (our son
watched by a stranger) into the dark theatre,

almost entirely empty but for a few seats occupied
by the lonely or wildly cinematropic,
where we munch on a chocolate biscotti and coffee,

and, all too tentatively, hold hands as the theatre
darkens and love's perpetual comi-tragedies
and little hurts unfold, in living color, acted out

by predictable legends, and we are vaguely happy
to be here, more or less intact in body and spirit,
but missing something, as all who dare twitch

beyond revery are missing something, and we would like
to think that we, too, might go to the Chinese doctor's
and be offered the magic herb with which tenderness

becomes, again, desire, and love could be cured
of its loveless, necessary, quotidian details—
yes, we might wish for it, as we might wish

for its comfortable, antithetical counterpart and come,
once more, to the place where too many things are true,
and always at once. And so, as the lights brighten

and we swallow the last bite of biscotti, the credits
reveal again the sources of those sad, happy, melancholy
songs we all love, and we should feel relieved to find

the line between art and life so beautifully navigated,
that we can still sneak off to the movies, in mid-
afternoon, knowing how easy it could have been for us

to be *possessed, ecstatic, unhappy, bad*—
if desire only wanted what desire had.

The Pact

People need not be glued together, when they belong together.
—Sigmund Freud

It's an old truth, that always lurks behind the curtain
of our fears, that people needn't be glued together
when they've gone deeply, when they're certain
that they're joined, when they belong together

Since people are inevitably glued together
when joined by fear, that fear of being two,
the fear that they might not belong together,
so they become a *me* and *me* instead of *you*

When joined by fear, this fear of being two,
a mocking tune that wants to triumph over life
as *me* and *you-as-me* instead of *me* and *you*
and sing one tune, the bisyllabic man and wife,

That seeming two, who'd like to triumph over life
by being one, by shaping every single tune
to chords so neat, the bi-syllabic hum of wife
and man that dims the stars, that tames the waxing moon

By seeming one, by shaping every single tune
the shape of fear, a dimmed container that revolves
around the stars, that tames the waxing moon
and dims the light, that dulls the old resolves

Until they're all the shape of fear, which then revolves
around the lie that makes two persons one,
dimming their lights, dulling what were two resolves
to one, a single spinning 'round the single sun

That they've become, unlike the two that must remain
when they've gone deeply, when at last they're certain
they're each a one, when neither bothers to complain
of that old truth, the one there waiting by the curtain.

A Walk on a Summer's Night

Not to go out in melancholy, or in rage,
or in a savage petulance
at what you cannot alter,
or full of some abysmal hierarchy
that excludes the human,
but to go out quietly, on a dark night
when the moon is a lit sickle
against the billowing fields,
and the cicadas trill out the marimbas
of their raspy voices, and all
your botched conceptions of what love is
have come back to haunt you;
to go out in a cognizant praise
of all that has brought you here,
because you have been blessed
with a story entirely your own,
because you are the cool elixir
of your own flames; to go out this way,
on a cool night shaken loose by a storm,
the air blanched with severity's afterthoughts
and your life only the pale diamond
you have mined for so long; to venture out
where no great exotica stirs in the woods
and the house you return to is not entirely yours,
and to know the night might suddenly go aflame
with stars you must first learn to share
before you call them your own.

"God Loves You, and So Do I"

Because it is what he says always, to anyone
(the dull girl in the tollbooth at the Triboro Bridge,
the wrong number who calls every night at nine,
the lamed colostomist who checks his colon,
even the stone-faced trooper who stops him
for driving 30 on the New York Thruway), my father,
the old Hassid from Frankfurt, passes through this life
in the vague service of some deific love,
and now I—having passed through hate
and back into love again—find myself saying it too
as we scud down the turnpike from Bar Harbor to Boston,
and a vague, generalized tenderness comes over me
in which I am the large man who carries his father
like unleavened bread, the one appointed
to shake the seeds of his ancestry into the day,
and, as we cruise down the highway
of tollbooths and diners, I become once more
the wild ideologue of my father's life—a man
waiving a white handkerchief into the air as he
plays the harmonica, calling out
to anyone who will listen:
"God loves you, and so do I."

Yin and Yang

My love is simple.
She sees a flower and she says:
flower. She sees the moon
and she whispers: *moon.*
Alone at night, under the deep stars,
we walk hand in hand by the river.
I say there is no justice
and she answers: *moon, moon,
stars, stars.* What shall I give her
by way of an answer? No longer young enough
to see the world as I wanted,
nor old enough to love it merely for what it is,
I pause, like a boat caught between tides
that must sing to its own moorings. Nothing,
myself included, is as I wanted it to be.
But I could get sentimental about all this,
I warn myself. So I take her again by the hand
until all the moonstruck faces have dispersed
into a sea of no large meanings. And we
walk on, like an old couple of mallards,
singing: *moon, moon, stars, stars.*

Bleibtreustrasse

Bleibtreustrasse: a street in Berlin, whose name is taken from the
German verb *treubleiben,* "to remain faithful."

I have sat on many streets,
in dark cafés at midday, and in dimly lit bars,
and know how neatly the heart seeks out
its original home, how easily we drift
to do the dark things done to us. Whose heart
has ever been wise enough for more goodness
than, unformed, it was granted? What boy
who's sniffed at his own body in search of treachery
hasn't grown treacherous? And who
hasn't listened, trembling,
while life cried out: *diversify,*
and love called back: *to specialize?*

How often have I walked out, ravenous,
with thoughts of betraying you? But,
time and again, the voice of some better being
cries out, and I see your rectifying face
in the mirror over the bar. O love,
who can resist being shamed into goodness
by his own late luck? And who can resist
the thrill of his own betrayals? Why
should I lie to you? It never ceases,
the longing. I stare out onto the street.
I turn my lustful eyes back toward the page.
I grieve for my one life. I praise my life.
I speak your name.

Half Full

Ahead the taillights of cars like raccoon's eyes
and, to the side, the hunched shoulders of the hills
through which we glide like a chute at leaf-fall's end

toward the elliptical grayness of November. Behind us,
the staccato gurgling of our son, mortality's clock,
wafts from the backseat, and, on the radio, an old tune,

I've got a peaceful, happy feeling, fills the half-
blissed air of the car, as I feel your hand putter
onto my knee and the old, familiar, bifurcated song

(*You are happy, you are sad, you are happy, you are
sad.*) begins to play again in my heart. All day,
the dense, unrelenting weight of our boy on my back,

we walked in the Indian-summered, New Hampshire hills
like actors in that old, oxymoronic story
of family romance. I stumbled once, and he poured

like a sack of potatoes from my back, hung by his heels
over an ominous-looking rock, then wept, then laughed
when he knew himself once more to be safe, and we went on,

up into the whitish, warm, revivifying air that hung
over the Presidentials, where we stopped, at a merely
human height, to share a banana and some cheese, and

he seemed so happy, our little boy, to have arrived
at something tangible, windswept, open to the long view,
the sun shimmying against his face like a blessing,

until we finally turned back, into the narrowing light
of late autumn, his small head sagging toward sleep
against the pack frame, the fatigue that approaches happiness

coming over us, the car heading south on the highway,
I've got a peaceful, happy feeling playing on the radio,
the full moon rising like love in the rearview mirror.

Risk

Why shouldn't a man be called hero by virtue of his natural death?
—Alane Rollings
"When Words Take Leave with Our Senses"

There are lives so safe you could weep for them,
sad things, flaccid and depleted, and we have all
dreaded them. But there are lives so dangerous

they shake all possible love from their limbs
and lie naked, bare, vulnerable
in the impossible air of their own imaginings.

Once I met a man who drove motorcycles
over ravines for a living, who said, "Love
is for chickens." I felt my own feathers tremble

as he spoke, partly thinking him right. Now,
I tremble to think what must have become of him,
with his Icarus-eyes and his scarred body

of untethered singing. As for myself, I've given up
all engines to the otherworldly, and come to believe
Calvino was right: *the best we can do is to avoid*

the worst, laughing and singing as we go. Last night,
I felt thick with courage, and, taking my wife
and young son in my arms, told them I loved them.

I was trembling as I spoke, and felt like a man
about to ride a motorcycle over a ravine. It
reminded me again that risk, like everything,

is relative and specific, that we all go
to our deaths in our own brave way. It reminded me
that this was all the risk I could tolerate,

all the risk I would ever need.

15

The Bear

Last night I dreamt I was a bear
And the moon was out, and the lake was clear,
And I got the better of an age-old fear
And took dominion everywhere.

Last night I dreamt I donned the skin
Of a dark brown coat that shimmered in the night
And I grew hairy with the darkness of my fright
And suddenly fierce, was fiercely masculine.

Last night I dreamt my father dead,
That man whom life defeated ere I could.
I emerged, all bloodied, from the darkened wood
And placed an unheard blessing on his head.

Last night I dreamt I was a man
Who loved his wife, who overcame his fear
And kissed her, from her small toe to her ear,
As only sons of deadened fathers can.

Last night I dreamt, I dreamt I was a bear
And, as my own son whimpered in the night,
I gave voice to an age-old, stifled fright
And put my bear hair everywhere.

A Prayer for My Son
for Noah

Little bird,
small sacred flake
that has fallen from the heat
of my longings, what
shall I wish for you today?

The day dawns
and you wake, singing
your hieroglyphic little tune
of gurgles and *da-da*s. I go
to gather you up in my arms
and the churning pistons of your legs
bicycle up into the early light
as if happiness were inevitable
as morning, as if life were merely a road
to pedal down. Tit-eager,
the small locomotive of your mouth
snakes through these rooms,
finding a world built only for you.

O little elf, not really mine,
but carrying my face
into the next life, hold on
to your hungers, hold on
to delight. And, sooner or later,
when sadness and disappointment creep
like a slow flood into your life,
may you yet grow wise—
but through passionate eyes.

The Difference between a Child and a Poem

If you are terrified of your own death,
and want to escape from it,
you may want to write a poem,
for the poem might carry your name
into eternity, the poem
may become immortal, beyond flesh
and fashion, it may be read
in a thousand years by someone
as frightened of death as you are,
in a dark field, at night,
when he has failed once again at love
and there is no illusion with which to escape
the inward pull of his own flesh
against the narrowing margins of the spirit.

But if you have accepted your own death,
if you have pinched daily the corroborating flesh,
and have passed the infinite gravestones
bearing your name, if you know for certain
that the day will one day come
when you will gaze into the mirror in search of your face
and find only a silence, then
you may want to make a child, you may want to push
the small oracles of flesh forward
into some merely finite but lengthening story,
you may want to toss your seed into the wind
like a marigold, or a passion fruit, and watch
as a fresh flower grows in your place, as your face
inches onto another face, and your eyes
slip down over your cheeks onto the forehead
of your silenced, speakable future.

And, then, when you are done with all that,
you may want to write a poem.

II

The Wages of Grief

To me alone there came a thought of grief;
A timely utterance gave that thought relief,
And again I am strong.
—William Wordsworth
"Ode: Intimations of Immortality
from Recollections of Early Childhood"

Ordinary Heartbreaks

To think that we could have had an ordinary family life with its bicker-ing, broken hearts and divorce suits! There are people in the world so crazy as not to realize that this is normal human existence of the kind everybody should aim at. What we wouldn't have given for such ordi-nary heartbreaks!

—Nadezhda Mandelstam
Hope Against Hope

The day dawns, and what to do with your one body?
At the door, there are no police.
You are of no great danger
to the tribe you live among.
Every crime language can commit
has already been licensed
toward some greater profit.
You look for a place for your rage,
the guile and pucker of it,
and only the faces of those you sleep with
are able to move you. Sweet world,
you think, with no place for the tragic
but your own house. So you make a mess
wherever mess allows. Suddenly,
a loud rapping on the door rouses you
from your reveries. Someone you love
is coming to get you. Unshackled,
you move slowly toward the door.
You feel a revolution coming,
your own four walls trembling.

For H., Dead in a Car at Thirty-eight

Today I blessed every little thing in the world
for its grace and its horror, and its sadness
and its reluctant love. I blessed the grass and the rain.
I blessed my sick and demented stepmother. I blessed the stars
that did not appear in the heavens last night, and I blessed
the stars that will appear in some heaven I will never live
to discover. I blessed my wife and my eight-week-old son,
who have come into my life against all the miserable odds,
and in whom, should I die in my bed tonight, I will have known
a sufficient happiness to make all sadness the good price
of its own redeeming. I blessed everything that is living
and whole, because you are dead, and, last time I saw you,
you were nearly a happy man, a man off in a car who had
published a book, wanting to be free of his own encumbrance.
Let me say it now: *I hardly knew you, and have no claim
to write this.* I even turned you down once for a job,
felt a twinge of envy when you told me your *sail* had become
a *sale.* There's nothing fair about it, let me tell you,
and now I am sitting here, feeling blessed because you're dead
and I'm still alive, sniffing the battered flowers, praising
the dark, fickle gods, hearing the same voice
calling *not me* that must have called it to you.

Letters Floating around Ellis Island

Today I was thinking about the millions of letters
that must still be floating around Ellis Island—
of Mrs. Rubin, the butcher's widow, who lost her *witz*

when she disembarked from Bialystok, of Mr. Slavin,
whose *ski* was taken from him when he arrived from Kiev,
of the millions of *steins* and *thals* and *bergs* and *schlags*

that are still floating in those waters, and of what
they must be thinking these days in late April
when the moon hangs like a tired sickle in the sky

and the earth trembles from all its corners like
an old sheet, and even the once-simple syllables
of men and women do not know, anymore, their place

in the wide world of flux. I think of those letters
floating like flotsam in that dimmed sea, and of all
they have survived during their shaken hours—

the kelped and sewaged light; the harsh embrasure
of cold ships; the ransacked air of old bottles and smoke
that must, these many years, have surrounded them;

the deaths, even, of the larger names they fell from.
Sometimes, when all hope seems to fall from my life
like a syllable ripped from a name at Ellis Island,

I think how they must rise into the dank air like songs
even the dead can sing from their old beds of longing,
how they are willing to stand for the old ways in a

vast sea of hype and incontinence, how they are able
to forgive everything over the wild din of all that has
fallen from them. I think of those syllables each day,

when my heart grows heavy as a stone and I look up
to ponder what survives in the end: the floating *witz,*
the ever-rising *berg,* the revivifying *thal.*

The Night the Dancing Died
April 19, 1968

The night Martin Luther King was shot,
we were all set to shimmy and do the snake
with the bronze girls and beautiful dark boys
at Gentleman Joe's in Binghamton, New York.

We were young and still beyond the easy hate
of class, or race, or purpose, or a job,
just a bunch of gangly, wide-eyed kids
with greased hips and a measure of be-bop,

Who wanted our souls to shuffle along the floor
to old Smokey Robinson and the Supremes,
and to dream of our bodies before the plague
of mindfulness and ambition had arrived.

We still dreamt of such a possible world
in which all things were equal when you danced,
where you could hear it through the grapevine of the songs:
the great mistake that set a man against a man.

But then, in some dark Memphis of the night,
a shot rang out, heard on all our streets
and suddenly our dancing feet were turned to clay,
our swiveling hips fell back into our chairs

And all that great equality the body sought
went burning in the chilly April air.

Elegy for My Mother: The Days

Betty Blumenthal
July 5, 1907–September 25, 1959

1. Prologue

It has been twenty-five years, now,
since you passed from this life,
and I wanted to pause for a moment
to finally grieve for you, because I am tired
of grief spent in the wrong places,
because I have spent half my biblical years
in a false rage, railing
at the wrong sources, self-preoccupied
against my own judgment, ungenerous
to those I've most loved
from the sheer pain of losing you.
So I will write, now, these words
as a final farewell, an epilogue to loss,
and kiss you again, body
that was taken from me, as I had wanted to then
but was not allowed, as I would allow
my own son, should he suffer the same fate,
to kiss his mother for the last time,
and so to be able to let go of grief,
as I will allow myself
(who have become mother to my own life)
to let go, to utter
this long-simmered exorcism of grief
into the air and be done with it,
as I will dedicate these words
to all I have hurt in your name,
and to myself, whose silenced grief
brought more grief into the world,
and to my own son, who shall yet issue
from my seed, breaking the curse of you,
breaking the curse of my impotent father
and of my father's father, breaking forever
the dark cycle of losses and angers
that your dying brought, bringing you
to life again in the name of life,

in the name of this, which I speak now,
that it may remain silent
for the rest of my days.

2. Sunday: The White Pail

You were sitting on the bed with my father.
It was late September.
The bedspread was a dark burgundy. The sun
was hovering like a lozenge over Fort Washington Avenue.
I had walked down the hill from my aunt's house
and was sitting alone in the living room, reading. Suddenly
I heard a sound like the cry of a stifled bird
coming from behind the bedroom door. I went on my tiptoes,
and opened the door. You were there, on the bed with my father.
You were holding his hand. In the other hand,
my father was holding a white pail. It was the same pail
my grandmother used to urinate in. But now
it was you, your head held like a spigot
over the white porcelain, who was using the pail.
A strange light was shining in your eyes.
You were holding your face above the pail,
vomiting into it. I didn't want to look,
yet felt a strange fascination with what I was seeing.
The vomit was deep green, like pea soup.
I couldn't help myself, and just kept standing there,
watching your throat heave like a clogged garden hose
over the pail. Suddenly, my father looked up
and saw me. He asked me to go into the living room
and get you some mints. I walked out of the room.
The mints were there, where they had always been,
in the Biedermeier cabinet you brought from Germany.
They were in a small, silver tray
beside the Kiddish cups. They were white,
just as the pail was white. I took the tray
and went back into the bedroom. You had stopped
vomiting now, but the vomit was still there in the pail.
You smiled and took some mints from my hand.
Thank you darling, you said, *thank you darling.*
You spoke in English, the language I was thinking in.
I turned to walk out of the room. You were still
sitting there, on the bed, holding my father's hand.

26

Thank you darling, you said again. *Thank you.*
It was the last time I ever saw you, sitting up.

3. Monday: The Rented Bed

They came early in the morning.
Two men, dressed in white and black. They wheeled
the large bed silently into the corner of the room.
It stood there like a huge, white dinosaur, silent
as sleep. It stood in the same place
I had slept as a child, and dreamed of falling.
But now it was you who was falling, now it was you
who fell into the fresh sheets, white
as the pail had been white, clean as snow.
Suddenly, the house began filling with people,
strangers in dark suits carrying small black bags, relatives
I hadn't seen in a long time. I walked
into the room. I felt like a comma
between the long sentence of intruders
who went in and out of the apartment all morning.
I wanted to turn the large crank at the foot of the bed and make
your head go up again. There was something fun about turning it,
like yanking water from a deep well, helping it to rise.
But you wouldn't rise. All the rising
had gone out of you, and you just lay there,
like an old boxer too tired to get up
after being knocked down for the last time.
Still, I kept turning the crank
until you nearly looked right into my eyes.
Leaves were falling from the trees
along Fort Washington Avenue. It was Monday,
September 21, 1959, in what was not the Year of our Lord.

4. Tuesday: Our Illness

Like a husband
taken to bed with the couvade
of his wife's birthing,
I woke, sick in my own flesh
with the thought of you.
I got out of my bed, like a fever
carrying a body, and walked back

into your room. You just lay there,
perfectly still, a large spider's web of tubes
running from all sides of you like cables
into some heavenly battery. I stood at the door
and stared, as though scouring the heavens
in search of a galaxy. I waited and waited.
But nothing rose. Nothing rose
except for a small armada of bubbles
into the glass beside you. The bubbles rose
into the dense liquid, like the last breath
of a drowning swimmer, like words
trying to say: *I am still here, son.*
I am still here.

5. Wednesday: Your Last Words

For weeks after you died,
I asked everyone who had been near you those last days
when they had last heard the sound of your voice.
I must have already known
that the voice was the heart's harp,
and wanted to know what chord, in the end,
had issued from yours. All day,
we had eked, you and I, our illnesses
into the feverish air. Now it was nighttime.
All day I had stayed in bed, mimicking you.
But now I rose, opening the bedroom door,
and—as I stood there watching—I felt
as if I were standing on a threshold
to somewhere I had never been. I felt
as if I were *your* mother, as if I myself
were a woman. You just lay there
on the high bed, cranked nearly down,
your eyes half open. I went in
and stood beside you. I could hear
your breath rising, like a wounded bird's,
from beneath the blanket. I could see
your right arm extending
into its circuitry of sugar. I placed
a small, warm hand on your arm.
Your eyes fluttered. I whispered,

as softly as I could, as though not wanting
to wake someone: *Good-night, Mom.*
There was a long silence. It seemed
like my words were passing to another place,
somewhere very far away. You opened your eyes,
as if you had suddenly been called back
from somewhere you were eager to get to.
I felt two fingers curl, ever so lightly,
around my own. At first you said nothing.
But then, as if by a heroic effort,
your lips began to move. It seemed like hours
before a word finally came. *Good-night, darling,*
I heard you say, *Good-night darling—*
words that would echo for years
through my silenced life.

6. Thursday: Your Eyes

All morning I begged them to let me enter the room. *Later,*
they kept saying. *Later, later.* All morning
I listened to the sound of the bedroom door
opening and closing, opening and closing.
I could hear them descending on you—the neighbors,
your brother Berthold, my father's sisters, a flotilla of doctors
with their little black bags, the rabbi
with his assorted *brochas.* Our house was a nest
of death and, like bees arriving to gather pollen,
they came to gather around you. After I begged
all morning to enter, someone came and led me
to the bedroom door. I remember looking
at the hallway clock. It was two in the afternoon.
Opening the door, I saw the burgundy bedspread again.
I was afraid, at first, to turn my head
to the large ghost of the bed where you lay. Finally,
though, I *did* turn my head. And what I saw terrified me.
Your eyes, glazed as if coated with shellac, were wide open,
staring up at me. Years later, in my hunger
for the mock-coherence of metaphor, I watched two Chinamen
pull a Northern Pike from the St. Lawrence River
and, in the death struggle of that huge fish, saw again
those eyes as I saw them now. But now I had nothing
with which to compare them, and—looking

29

as if into a deep, bottomless well—I looked,
for the first time, Death in its very face and called it:
Mother. But you didn't answer. Like a trapped fly
dissolving into a spider's web, you just lay there,
the mute syllables of another country issuing from you.
Mother, I called out again, *Mother, Mother.*
Twenty-five years later, I would still be speaking
whatever words would come to me
into the long silence of what you answered.

7. Friday: The Empty Bed

I woke to a commotion of rabbis
and the scent of dying. Death itself
had slinked through the halls like a serpent
during the night, choking the breath from you.
Now, returned to your original innocence,
you were merely a body again, and I could not overcome
the desire to kiss you. I wanted to go into the room
where your body lay, body from which I had never fed,
body whose naked breasts I had never seen, and kiss
the body good-bye. I wanted to hold you, mother
of no milk, one last time, to place my mouth
against your mouth and breathe the life back into it.
I started toward the room. Living hands restrained me.
Living voices said: *Not yet. Not yet.* What else
could I do, a man's hurt in a boy's body? I waited,
listening to the sound of doors opening and closing,
wheels rolling down the hallway, the whispered voices
of strangers. I knew what they must be doing,
but couldn't believe it. *Wait,* they told me.
Just wait. We'll let you in. No one knew
what they were doing. No one knew
how long a man mourns, mutely,
for a child's missed mourning. Suddenly,
the small concertina of wheels and doorbells stopped.
The whole house became terribly silent. Someone
came into the room to get me.
It was my friend Raymond's father, Kurt,
our family's accountant. I was crying.
You can go in now, he told me. *You can
go in now.* Slowly, I turned the knob

to the bedroom door. I turned my eyes
from the burgundy bedspread to where I hoped
I would find you. The bed was still there. The sheets
were still perfectly white, as though not even death
had been able to soil them. But you were gone. You were
not even a body anymore. For the next twenty-five years,
I would be blowing kisses
into the emptiness of what I found there.

8. Saturday: The Pink Nightgown

All day I watched the baseball playoffs on TV.
Small processions of grief echoed like commercials
through the house. The low stools were recalled
from their closets like pinch hitters. For months,
I had emptied my sadness into you. But now
that they had taken your body, I no longer wanted
to know the grief of bodies. I wanted, merely, to think
of strikeouts and passed balls, the living heroics
of the great catch. That night, the ballgame won,
the mourners risen from their low stools
to return to their houses, my father called me
into the room where you had died. I stood
before the Biedermeier dresser, eyes to the ground,
as he bent to open the bottom drawer. There—
neatly folded as if waiting, still, for your body—
was your pink nightgown. Slowly, my father
lifted the nightgown to his lips. I watched it rise
like a loaf of bread in my father's hands,
moving toward me. He whispered a blessing in Hebrew.
Then, instead of the body I had so wanted to kiss,
my father held the empty nightgown against my face
and whispered: *Gib unsre Mama*
einen letzen kuss, Give our mother
one last kiss. Terrified, I closed my eyes
and made the puckering sound of a feigned kiss
as I felt the cold silk rising to my lips.
Ever since then, I have turned
my living face away from women's eyes.

9. Sunday: The Funeral

It was a beautiful day.
I was at my friend Raymond's,

where they had sent me. I could hear
the church bells along Fort Washington Avenue.
I looked out the window and saw a long serpent
of black cars lined up along the curb, a procession
of shoulders wrapped in fur entering them. I couldn't keep myself
from watching as they drove off. I tried to look
into the windows of each of the cars. I didn't want
to miss, again, your body. Then, suddenly,
I found myself sitting on the floor with Raymond,
laughing wildly. I laughed and laughed,
until my whole stomach hurt, but I couldn't stop.
Your mother has just died, I said to myself. *How
can you laugh this way?* I've forgotten
everything else about that day, though I've tried
for years to remember. I've forgotten
when they came home, what they said, whether or not
the rabbi took me into my room again to say
it was all for me. But I remembered, always,
that long, wild, belly-aching laugh
and the long serpent of black cars, and wondered
whether, had I wept then, I might have been spared
the long, silent weeping since. I wondered
whether, had I wept then,
I might have wept for real.

10. Monday: The Low Stools

Now your body was gone from the whole house equally.
The white bed was gone. The pink nightgown was gone.
The long serpent of black cars was gone. Even
the pious rabbis—they, too, were gone.
Only the low stools ventured out like understudies
from the shadows of their waiting. I went back to my room,
convinced for many years that you would return to me,
having never fully seen you gone. But I have sat, now,
on my low stool long enough, calling grief
a kind of happiness in your name, hoping to breathe
the life back into you. I am tired, now,
of the low stools and empty nightgowns, tired
of sucking at your nonexistent breasts. Dead woman,
mother of no blood, yet mother as surely
as feeling brings blood into the world, *you are dead,*

32

dear woman, you are dead. So be gone, finally,
as you have been gone all these years. Take,
at last, the heavens for your home . . .
And give back the earth.

11. Thanksgiving, 1984: Your Grave

Now I stand near your grave in a man's body.
I look out over the low hills
of New Jersey, the state
I was born in, over the vast valley
of stone slabs, white
as your empty bed was white,
white as the pail into which you began
to pour back your life. In all directions,
the names of my childhood—*Heilbronn,
Schoenbach, Marx, Meyer, Hirsch, Guttman,
Dingfelder, Katzenstein*—call out
their cold litanies of stone,
old *daveners* reunited once more
in a synagogue of hedges, a vast democracy
of marble and flowers.

Then, in the near distance,
as if in an aisle seat,
I find you:
> BETTY BLUMENTHAL
> nee Gern
> 1907–1959

etched into the glistening stone.
I find you, mother of no body,
mother of affections but not flesh,
beside your own mother, who—
in one of those wild inversions
that makes myth of a family—
followed you here:
> JOHANNA GERN
> nee Neumark
> 1876–1966

and I understand once more why I am
what I am: a man who must bear
himself anew into the world each day
by speaking his life. I see

how the tidal surge of grief must come ashore,
how the force that drives no water for so long
must well up inside the tangible body of flesh
until a new wave rises behind it. I see how,
for almost thirty years, I have dipped
the wafer of my own life into your dying
and partaken of it; how, brought
into the world to save you, I can save
no one, not even myself.

I place my black book against your headstone.
Something very much like speech
rises from the water behind you.
I weep you dead. And you are dead.

12. Epilogue: The Threshold

I stand once more at the threshold
to your room. Once more, I can see
the high bed in the corner, your body

lying on it. I summon the relentless
goddess, Mnemosyne, to my side, and feel
my own body turn once more into the body

of a young boy. I see your wide eyes
staring up at me from the high bed,
head that can move no more, lips

that can speak no more. I stand there,
at the place I was kept from entering,
and look in at you. Years of my life

pass before me. I lift my too-long-
hampered legs and step over the threshold.
I step from the long corridor of grief

into the room, and stand beside you.
I place my fingers against your face.
look into the deep, unseeing wells

of your eyes, and stare Death in its
literal face. *Hello, Death,* I say,
I have come for you now. Hello, Death.

I have come for you for real. Thirty years
of my life congeal into that single instant.

Hundreds of women I could not kiss,

hundreds of women I could not see, merge
into the dying light of your eyes. I lower
my face toward your face. I lower my lips

toward your lips and plant on them, now,
that long-belated kiss—the kiss
of death, the kiss all life comes from.

1984–1990

III

The Wages of Goodness

Virtue is bold, and goodness never fearful.
—Shakespeare
Measure for Measure

United Jewish Appeal

My grandmother was eighty-nine and blind
and I was a young boy hungry for quarters,
so, in the waning light
of Sunday afternoons, my parents gone,
I would ring the doorbell
(my friend Raymond smirking
from behind the stairwell) and listen
for the slow shuffle of slippers
in the hall, the soft thump
of her body against the closet.

She would come to the door,
my parakeet Jerry trapped in her hairnet,
stammering a "Who's there?" in minimal English,
between the chain and the doorjamb,
and, without hesitancy or shame,
in a cracked, mock-Hassidic voice,
I'd answer: "United Jewish Appeal,"
swaying my hand, like a small plane
moving over an airstrip, toward her.

She would open the door—tentative,
timid, charity having won out over terror—
and reach a palm out into the hallway,
the way she reached out under the candles
to bless me on Sabbath. "My daughter . . .
she would stammer, "she is not home now,"
poking her eyes like Borges into the vastness.
A better heart than mine was
might have stopped there, but I was a boy
ravenous for malteds and baseball cards,
so I repeated the words of my small litany,
"United Jewish Appeal," and reached my hand out again
until it almost touched the blue print of her smock.

All the while my parakeet sat there,
dropping small coils of bird shit onto her hair
until she retreated again down the long yellow hallway,
reading the braille of the walls
with her hands. And I would wink
at my good friend Raymond behind the stairwell

39

when the rattle of change clanged out
from my parents' bedroom, and we heard again
the slow sweep of her feet, and, at last,
the shiny fruits of cleverness and hunger
fell into my palm, and my grandmother Johanna,
the parakeet still flapping like a crazed duck
in her hairnet, closed the door behind her,
leaving me and my friend Raymond
to frolic off into the sun-licked,
agnostic streets of Washington Heights,
full of the love of grandmothers
and of change, forever singing the praises
of the United Jewish Appeal.

Cherries

After Auschwitz, it's been said, it's no longer possible
to write about cherries. But the cherries were there,
across from the abandoned lavender oil extraction stove,

surrounded by fields of poppy and thistle and lemon balm
and thyme, in the old, nearly abandoned village of Montmorin,
once controlled by the Moors, and, when we went to pick them,

the air smelled of lavender, rosemary and linden blossom
and my son was sleeping against the breast of my wife,
who looked especially beautiful in the late light

of Alpes de Haute Provence, and the cherries were delicious
against our pallets, turning our tongues a purplish red,
their juice dripping down our chins, the magpies hovering

over us like priests, the crows pirating the hayfields,
and I found myself with no choice but to bless
the ambiguous God of cherries and magpies and children

and marriage, to bless the strange God of my eccentric
mother-in-law Yvette, gathering cherries high in the trees,
and to curse the dark God of Auschwitz and Treblinka

and Birkenau and Dachau, relishing the taste of cherries
in my mouth, refusing to believe they are the same God.

Tongues

To make the frozen circumstances dance, you have to learn to sing to them their own music.

—Karl Marx

I turn to my cold blood
in the language of blood.

And in the shrill, ivory tones of neglect,
I sing to the widening penumbra of my neglect.

In the incoherent babble of the child,
I return to my childhood.

And in the sharp, unfeeling syllables of betrayal,
I renounce my betrayals.

Soon,
I will be a master of many tongues,

a Pentecostal rabbi chanting to the ghosts
of all my infidelities as they fall from the heavens.

And I will skate by
on the ice that has become my life—

whispering to the moon
in the language of the moon,

beckoning to the stars
in the voice of the stars,

waiting for the mute tides to ripple
beneath my rubbery legs

as I stoop to address the ice
in the cold, brackish language of water,

and of salt.

Emilio Roma Is Dead
In memoriam, Emilio Roma III

Yours were the sexy subjects:
whether an *ought* could ever imply an *is,*
how two lovers engaged in the same immodest act of love
are always thinking in different ontologies,
how whatever it is that we think is there
may only be there, as The Bishop suggested,
in the hungry eyes of some lonely perceiver.

You were the prince of phenomenology
and touch football: everywhere you went,
dazed, impressionable eyes of young girls followed.
Young, romantic, ravenous for reference,
we watched you glide onto the campus
like some beautiful raptor, a man determined
as long as he lived to resemble a monument.

How terrified you must have been,
holding death so firmly in your beautiful body,
knowing the cool drumming of your existential heart
wouldn't beat forever in its mere house of flesh
and borrowed continuing. Lame, diabetic, angina-pectorised,
my rickety father seemed certain to precede you. But now,
twenty years and thousands of jogged miles later,

An old classmate tells me you are dead
and I look at my own aging body, a bruised thing
waning its way into afternoon. I see you still,
a man-child in black jeans and sneakers,
carrying a notebook marked *Ethics* up to the podium.
My father, that true survivor, smiles down at you
from his patched nest of deaths and resurrections.

You are there now, Emilio, where no *ought*
has ever implied an *is*—fixed for all time
in the gaze of our foremost philosopher,
that last perceiver.

Say

for Wendy Parsons

Say you have always wanted to be someone,
someone brave, perhaps, or lighter than air,
someone who has trapped tigers in Borneo or has flown,

effortlessly, in the sweet balloon of his own desires,
someone for whom the wind itself subsides, and who,
in the relinquished dreams that fall from him

like petals from a deracinated flower, is the many things
he has always wanted to be. Say you have wanted to be
this someone so badly that you have *been* to Borneo

(though without tigers) and you have *lived* in air
(without flying), and you have survived on the shore
of some exaggerated bravery like a dumb fish, revved

your engines too many times on the cool runway of your
own imaginings. But each time—there waiting for you
when you return, like the good servant who knows no rancor—

is the unimbellishable truth of who you are, the grinch
of your own facticity that sits by the window
and is strangely content to live on the unspectacular plains

of his exotica: some wild Serengeti he needs not travel to,
but whose beasts must nevertheless be contended with
and fed, and are equally dangerous and out to kill,

and are out to teach humility, to whatever
gets in their way, in whatever guise.

First Snow: Cambridge, Massachusetts

The trees cough up a plenitude of starlings
and the day, suddenly sheeted
with an almost-innocence of white,

Calls out to you as if it were a bed
and you the minstrel who invented music.
You walk out into an un-prescience of bicycles,

(Wedded to parking meters by encyclicals of ice)
into the early slosh-work of first pedestrians
and it is as if God's pillow had burst during the night,

Bathing the world in a downdrift of feathers. *What
to do with the day?* So mortal you could weep
for the mere humanness of your celebrations,

You walk out toward the river, into a stillness
of no boats, a world demonstrably without wars
or famine, without injustice. Pines bow

To the servitude of snow, people are donning
the old prosthetics of their legs, the good
intentions of bakers are leavening the air.

Everywhere you look, things are shagged
with the white veneer of the heavenly,
peppered only by birds. But soon (you know)

A terrible seriousness will reclaim the day,
though for now it is merely a triumph
of good intentions, a clean slate with only you

And this tinsel of first snow to write on it,
as if such a plenitude could rule the world,
or snow could, or the starlings in earnest.

Five Answers for Sacvan Bercovitch

1. When will we meet again?

In a drizzle, maybe, in the sun,
well before my young son Noah has turned one.

Before (I hope) George Bush invades Iraq,
before the trees are blooming once again in Rock Creek Park.

After Thanksgiving, or so it looks right now,
before the winter storms make birch trees bow.

Before the snows are gone, in wintered sun,
before our backs are bent, before we're done.

2. Did Buster Douglas throw the fight?

One man gets up, another man falls down,
some men play victor, others play the clown.

Evander punched, and Buster hit the turf,
some men are brave, while others lose their nerve.

Who is to say which is the wiser course?—
to die with guts, or live full of remorse.

I sense that, with those butterflies still in his head,
our flattened Buster thought: *Why, better rich than dead.*

3. Why does S. pick such strange men?

Though I myself have been on many dates,
why should I try to better dear old Yeats:

It's still quite clear that lovely women eat
(like men) a crazy salad with their meat.

4. Why are the just so often defeated, and the unjust triumphant?

We know what Job once said about his task,
and what poor Esau found, and Abel too.
And we've been patient long enough to ask
for punishment for evil Christian, Moslem, Jew.

But who are we, I wonder, to make sense
of questions whose resolve has long defied

our silent betters, seeking recompense
for their good deeds, only to ponder suicide.

The world's just too inscrutable for those
(like you and me) who'd like virtue to live
in tandem with the beautiful and just, and who suppose
that *overlook*'s not quite the equal of *forgive*.

But here's the world—a mystery to us,
yet somehow still so beautiful and strange,
that simply won't reward the virtuous,
who spend their kindness. Others keep the change.

**5. *Where were we when the heavens were created and
the morning stars sang for joy?***

Fast asleep, no doubt, in some still-quiet, safer place,
our souls still waiting for a human face.

Not yet enwombed, entombed, entwined,
not yet at odds with the divine.

Where were we, Saki, on that fateful day
when some learned singing, others how to pray?

October 1990

47

Meditation on Politics at the Quabbin Reservoir

for Joseph Duffey

All day there has been no peace
from the species that hates its own silence
so I have come here now,

where the dandelions are mere ghosts
of their former selves, and the reservoir
tongues its way onto the rocks, to find

once more the peace of my own stillness,
a small omen of the enduring clarities
that will contain our epitaph (*we saw things*

for what they were, but acted in spite of them).
But now, for a small moment, it is a world
rife with warblers and incipient eagles,

a stillness at midday we can detour
out of the usual urgencies to come upon.
Yet, even here, I have in me a bit

of the non sequitur: evil thoughts
I cannot disown come upon me, as much mine
as the fine purity I came here in search of.

Sullied thing that I am, I see this day now
for the fine meadow I lie on, and the cruel havoc
that buzzes beneath it. Meadow was never our metaphor,

friend, nor pure light—only the confluence of good
and evil where we meet to become this: possessors
of a merely partial purity, a purely human one.

The Geologist

Grand Canyon, May 1988

He had made a life of stone:
of sandstone and basalt,
of dolomite and shale
and the wild permutations of schist.
Siltstones spoke to him
and the hard crystals of metamorphic rock:
His life became a history
of sediments and erosions,
of deep strata fissured and faulted
into a great transmutation
of flakes and embering chips.
Nights, he spoke in his sleep
of downcutting rivers,
primordial sea floors
crumpled and forced into islands,
only to resubmerge as wandering continents.
He could see the veins of magma
shooting up through the mountain ranges,
he could feel the great unconformities,
the missing pages and sentences
of subsidences and diastems.
All that he loved of the world
was stone and water, water and wind,
Cambrian and Paleozoic. But he was not
a stupid man, by any stretch
of the imagination. For he never mistook
pyrite for true gold. He wasn't fool enough
ever to take gneiss for granite.

Buying Baseball Cards at Forty-two

for Marilyn Levine

It is because I wanted to see again their faces,
they who were once gods, that I go now, on this warm,
April-suggestive night in late winter, to the corner drugstore

And follow the forever pink-scented scent of bubble gum and childhood
to the cashier's stand, where they are still there, in thickened,
Ninety-nine-cent packages of thirty-four cards, beside the hockey stars
    and fullbacks.

Yet tonight, as I head home to my own not-yet-upright son
and, trembling, tear open the package, they are somehow smaller,
gumless, flawed, less awesomely manly than I remember them.

They seem, in fact, more like the self-overblown, near-children
I teach, and I am forced to smile at my own errored ascendency,
my non-recognition of names and places. *Baines, Lieberthal,*

Larkin, Lefebrve, young men from far off, once un-baseballed towns
called *Toronto, Seattle, Minneapolis, Houston,* I look down at them,
gazing back from their cocksure, switch-hitting, deathless stances,

and the happy litany of my own pantechnicon echoes again, singing
Snider, Furillo, Kluzewski, Kubek, reminding me that the immortals
have always been with us in the Ebbets Fields, Polo Grounds,

Wrigley Stadiums and Comiskey Parks of some irreplaceable venue,
and that they, too, have gone the way of all gods,
as I, heading home to my son, have gone the way of all sons.

Ark

for Peggy and Howard Nemerov

*All the creatures, by pairs and by tribes, pour into his mind as into a
Noah's ark, to come forth again to people a new world.*

—Ralph Waldo Emerson
The Poet

My son plays with the ark you gave him.
In pairs and tribes, he pours
the plastic animals into the bathwater
and gurgles up toward me, smiling
his baby smile, as a large pair
of floating grey elephants
tremble, soap-soaked, downriver
like old tires, and the orange giraffe
does a *tour-jetté* around his happily slapping hand,
nearly mounting a diminutive white sheep.
Not yet does my little son know
of the enmity between woman and man, not yet
does he know how slow the bones are
to worship anything beyond themselves.
All future, he goes *ga-ga* over the grey,
white, purplish pairs of his namesake's house,
not knowing they are merely the offspring
of the end of all flesh, not knowing
how lonely he is sure to be among the blessed
and the just, among those who find grace
in the eyes of the Lord, who must be fruitful,
and multiply, who must replenish the earth.

Poem for My Father at Eighty-five after Cross-Country Skiing with My Nephew, Marlon, Age Seven

It is as the Good Book says: *he whom the gods love,*
they correct, so, amid spruce, fir, and pine
dusted with snow, we set out, he in his blue down suit

and the fiberfill gloves I bought him for Christmas,
I in my dark blue vest and red hat, pushing off
like two birds into the hills, gliding up and down

the deeply grooved tracks the others have left for us,
as I call out to him: *Suis-moi, mon ami,* and he follows,
imitating me, and I am part ache, part happiness

as he glides with such perfect, self-infatuated delight,
down the hill after me, and two beautiful women turn
in their tracks to watch, thinking I am his father,

loving the brisk, initiatory glee of it: this young boy
following a grown man like an imprinted duck,
waving his arms wildly into the air, bending his knees,

as I fill the white, wintry woods with applause,
calling out, *Tres bien, Marlon, magnifique! Champion!*
Then his cheeks grow pink with contentment and cold,

as we stop at a stump bathed in clear light,
where I help him off with his skis and we share a banana,
and now we are two men, full of our bodies and winter

and the half-jesting mockery of women, and now it is I,
father, who am the older man, and, like all men
raging to repeat themselves, shimmy only half-blissed

toward my own bettering, as I brush the snow
from this fatherless boy, all laughter now,
who must issue nearly alone into the half-lit,

half-darkening world of his manhood, and then
we are done eating, and a white sootfall of flakes
begins again, and I say: *On doit rentrer,*

les autres attendent, and we start back down the hill,
along the river's trickling glassflow, where I show him
les feuilles mortes de l'an dernier, and then

I am thinking, again, of you, with whom I could never
have done this, and, next thing I know, we arrive,
in the brilliant January light, at the waiting arms

of his mother, and my wife, and he looks back,
this boy who is now leading me out of the woods,
and cries out: *Nous arrivons!* And I half-weep

my way into their arms, these beautiful women,
pushing one foot in front of the other, planting
my poles like canes, loving what little I can,

turning my face toward the sun, correcting the world.

And the Wages of Goodness Are Not Assured

for Aharon Appelfeld

That Jacob stole his own brother's blessing
and lived to triumph from it there can be
no doubt, or that Cain slew the sleeping Abel

or that Job suffered so long amid the racked syllables
of his own believing, that the wages of goodness
are oblique and obscure, and not even assured

in some happy ending, all this should give us pause
when we contemplate the abstract justice
of some more perfect world, when we sift

through the dark lexicon of possible deeds
in search of some wished-for Eden where righteousness
is a large sequoia growing in a damp wood,

surviving drought and lightning storms, rising up
over the drone of its possible adversaries
as if there were no possible questioning

its heavenly arriving, as if the one recourse
to an empire of inevitable darkness were merely
a purposeful upreaching, a shaft of unending light

that finds its way over the contentious canopy
of all that diminishes it. No, it may be better
to remember Juliek, playing his violin

in the dank air of Buchenwald, how he saw
no other avenue out of the ghostly enterprise
but to keep playing, to keep guiding

the bow gently over the singing strings
while the dead were being heaped on the living
and the wages of goodness were being paid

in a more dubious currency, when the only thing left
for a man to do was just to keep playing like that,
keep singing into the light of this darkening world.